DATE DUE

LEADERS OF
ANCIENT ROME

AUGUSTUS The First
Emperor

LEADERS OF
ANCIENT ROME

AUGUSTUS The First Emperor

Fiona Forsyth

the rosen publishing group's
rosen
central

921
AUG
c\2003
23.95

Published in 2003 by The Rosen Publishing Group, Inc.
29 East 21st Street, New York, NY 10010

Copyright © 2003 by The Rosen Publishing Group, Inc.

First Edition

Library of Congress Cataloging-in-Publication Data

Forsyth, Fiona.
Augustus: the First Emperor / Fiona Forsyth.— 1st ed.
p. cm. — (Leaders of ancient Rome)
Includes bibliographical references and index.
ISBN 0-8239-3588-4
1. Augustus, Emperor of Rome, 63 B.C.–14 A.D.—Juvenile literature. 2. Emperors—Rome—Biography—Juvenile literature. 3. Rome—History—Augustus, 63 B.C.–14 A.D.—Juvenile literature. I. Title. II. Series.
DG279 .F67 2002
937'.07'092—dc21

                                        2001006261

Manufactured in the United States of America

CONTENTS

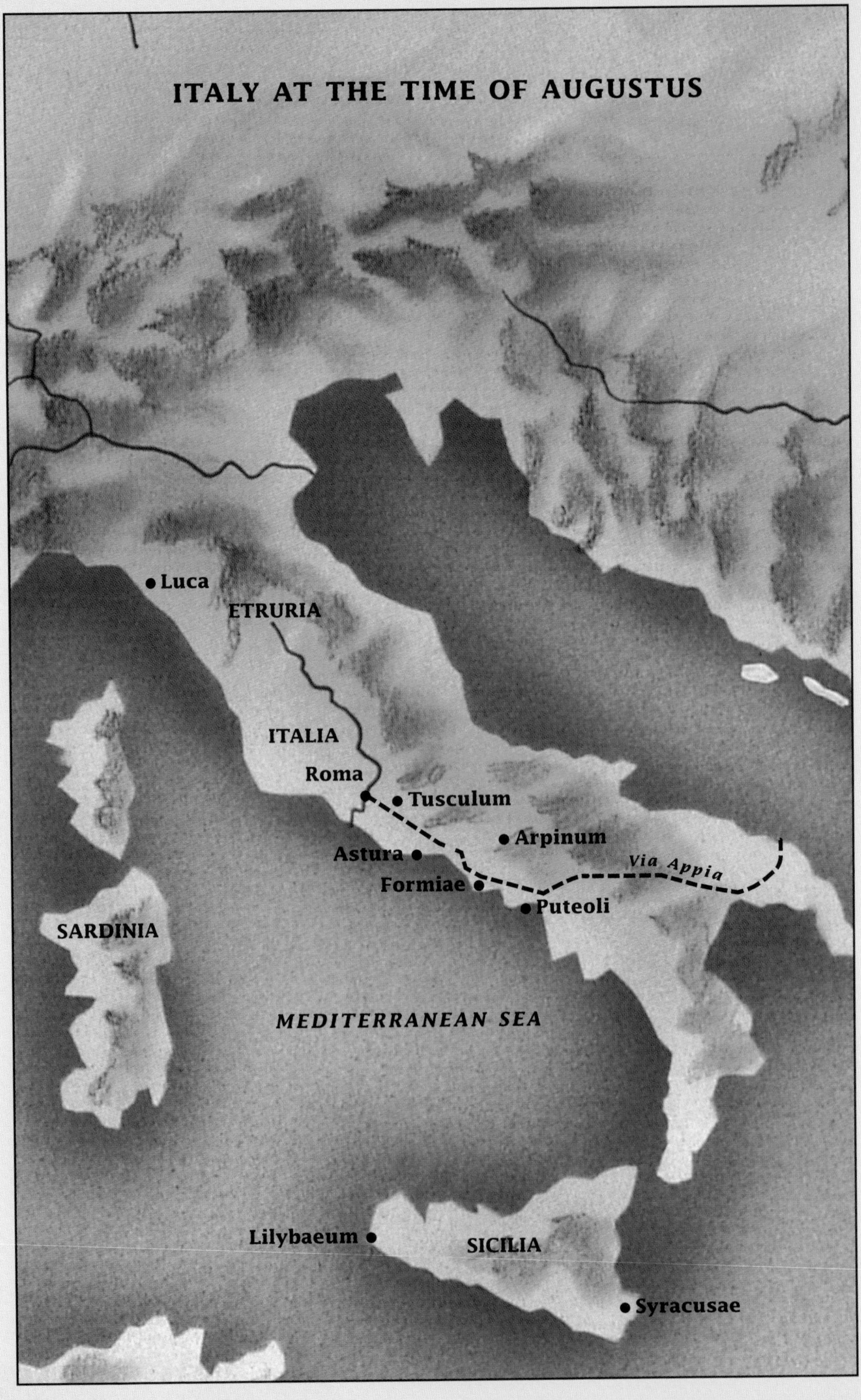

ITALY AT THE TIME OF AUGUSTUS

Luca

ETRURIA

ITALIA

Roma

Tusculum

Arpinum

Astura

Via Appia

Formiae

Puteoli

SARDINIA

MEDITERRANEAN SEA

Lilybaeum

SICILIA

Syracusae

INTRODUCTION

The Italian town of Nola lies inland from the Bay of Naples, tucked in behind the volcano Vesuvius. In AD 14, it was the scene of the death of a Roman nobleman. He was seventy-five years old, and he died in the same room of the same house where his father had died, seventy-two years earlier. He had made his farewells, asking his friends light-heartedly if they thought he had performed well in the comedy of life. He had kissed his wife and asked her to remember their marriage before dying easily and quickly, as he had wanted. It was picture-perfect, as Gaius Julius Caesar Octavianus Augustus, Rome's first emperor, pulled off yet another piece of brilliant publicity—his own death.

The man we call Augustus, first emperor of Rome, lived from

This statue of Augustus portrays him as an imperial military leader.

63 BC to AD 14. From the age of eighteen, when he became involved in politics, he lived a life carefully planned and orchestrated for its maximum effect on the Roman people. It is very tempting to wonder if Augustus had even planned his deathbed scene, down to the touching last words to his wife and friends. As you discover more about Augustus, you will realize that he was perfectly capable of this sort of planning.

Augustus made a huge difference to the world of ancient Rome. The historians call his time the Age of Augustus, and in this age Rome clothed herself in marble and made some of her leaders into gods. In fifty years, Augustus transformed himself and his city.

In 63 BC, when Augustus was born, Rome was what we call a republic. This word is derived from the Latin phrase *res publica*, which means "public affairs." No single person had too much power, and a complicated division of powers kept the republic safe and stable. Hundreds of years earlier in their history, the Romans had been ruled by kings, and the experience had not been a success. The Romans had been oppressed by some kings, threw them out, and vowed never to let them rule again. Instead, every year men were chosen in elections to fill the offices that kept the state running on a day-to-day basis. If you were male, an adult, and a citizen of Rome, you had the right to vote in these elections.

The men who held office were automatically admitted to the Senate, a sort of council with about 500 men in it. The Senate discussed public affairs and gave advice to the officers and the people of Rome about passing laws. Because you had to be rich and wellborn to become a candidate for office, the Senate was more powerful than a council that just gave advice. Being wealthy and knowing all the other wealthy people give you a clear advantage in practically any society. The Senate did not have things its own way all the time, however. Special groups of ten men, called tribunes, were chosen by the people every year to keep an eye on the Senate and make sure that the interests of the ordinary people of Rome were protected.

This system was beginning to break down when Augustus was born. Some individuals wanted more power for themselves and did not want to play by the rules. These individuals were able to maneuver and exploit the Roman political system by building power bases in its far-flung provinces. As Rome had grown from her foundation, traditionally dated at 753 BC, she had conquered many lands, which were then called provinces. At the time of Julius Caesar, these provinces stretched from modern Spain and France to Turkey and into North Africa. Roman officials would be sent to govern these provinces, and taxes would be raised and sent back to Rome. These provinces were controlled with a large army divided into legions. As legions were dispatched to areas of unrest, there was an opportunity for the commanders leading them to make themselves more powerful by building up a strong relationship with their troops. Once the soldiers owed more loyalty to an individual commander than to Rome, the commanders were in a position to make demands.

This naturally had a great effect on Augustus and his generation, for a change of this sort rarely comes about without violence. For the first eighteen years of his life, Augustus watched individuals build up their personal power and destroy the republican system. He saw politics turn violent. He saw civil war break out when he was thirteen years old, caused in part by his own great-uncle, Julius Caesar, who refused to give way to another general, Pompey. Fortunately for Augustus, Caesar won that particular struggle.

When Augustus was eighteen, Julius Caesar was given the unheard-of title *dictator perpetuus*, meaning "dictator for life." This was a very dangerous step for Julius Caesar to take, for the office of dictator in the Roman Republic was conceived of only as an emergency measure. It was supposed to be held for a maximum of six months so that a crisis could be dealt with and the republic returned to normal. By taking this title for life, Julius Caesar was undermining the republic and, some people said, aiming to make himself a king. This was the reason why men like Brutus and Cassius, who were colleagues and even personal friends of Caesar, felt that they had to assassinate him. They hoped that the republic would be restored, but they made a grave misjudgment. There were too many ambitious men who felt they could succeed where Caesar had failed.

THE GREAT-NEPHEW

In 63 BC, a young Roman politician called Gaius Octavius was doing very well for himself. He was climbing the ladder of offices that led to the top rung of Roman politics. This ladder was called the *cursus honorum*, and at the top was the office everyone hoped to get—consul. Gaius Octavius wasn't there yet, but he was likely to be a candidate for the office of praetor in a year or two, and after being praetor for a year you were rewarded with a governorship. As Rome had grown more powerful, she had conquered other lands around the Mediterranean and turned them into provinces of her empire. Officials got their first taste of provincial life when, after holding the praetorship, they governed a small province for a year before coming back to Rome and trying to be elected consul.

A bust of Augustus as a young man, when he was known as Octavius

Competition was strong for all these offices, but Gaius Octavius was confident of success. He was from a respectable family, he had money, and his wife, Atia, was related to the Julius family, one of the oldest in Rome. Atia's uncle, Julius Caesar, was also beginning to make a name for himself in politics, and Gaius Octavius looked to him for help up the *cursus honorum*. Gaius Octavius had all the connections he needed to make his way in Roman politics. To crown it all, on September 23, 63 BC, Atia gave birth to a son. Every Roman wanted a son to carry on the family name, so Gaius Octavius must have been very proud. The baby was named after his father, Gaius Octavius. He had two elder sisters, one of whom was a half sister from his father's previous marriage. The boy was especially close to his full sister, Octavia, and they remained close for the rest of their lives.

When young Gaius Octavius was four years old, his father died and his mother went on to marry Lucius Marcius Philippus, who became consul in 56 BC. Julius Caesar also took an interest in his young great-nephew. He had no son of his own, and the young Octavius was very likely to be adopted as his heir. As Julius Caesar moved into the final phase of his own struggle for power, Octavius was given a taste of what was in store for him. In 46 BC, at the age of sixteen, he went to Spain to join his great-uncle in one of the campaigns of the civil war. He so impressed Caesar that he decided to take the boy with him on his next campaign to Parthia, in Asia. Caesar had returned to Rome to make the arrangements for the campaign there, but he also had officers gathering and training troops at Apollonia, a town on the west coast of Greece. Gaius Octavius was sent there to observe the training of the soldiers and continue his education with the Greek teachers of Apollonia.

CAESAR'S HEIR

While he was in Apollonia, however, everything changed for Octavius. The news was brought from Rome that Julius Caesar had been killed by a group of conspirators led by his friend Marcus Brutus. Caesar's great-nephew was faced with a critical choice. Should he go back to claim his place as Caesar's heir, or should he wait in Greece to see what happened in Rome? If he returned to Rome without a clear idea of the situation, he might be walking into a very dangerous and violent situation. But if he waited, others might seize the initiative and put him on the sidelines, too young and inexperienced to matter. Octavius decided to return.

At this point, few people in Rome knew much about Octavius or even cared. At the age of eighteen, Roman men still had a long way to go before they achieved a position of authority or power, and they were expected to treat their elders with respect and wait their turn. Octavius knew he would have difficulty making people take him seriously, so he had to think of some unusual ways of attracting attention. He began with his name. He knew that Caesar had intended to adopt him and make him his heir. Caesar should have made all this clear in his will, but that was in the possession of Caesar's friend Mark Antony in Rome. Octavius decided to start calling himself Gaius Julius Caesar Octavianus. The "Octavianus" was to show that he had originally come from the

Octavius family, and modern historians find it useful to call him Octavian because it helps to distinguish him from his great-uncle. But the young man himself preferred the name Caesar. This was his first change of name, and it shows that he already knew the power of names and titles. Julius Caesar's old soldiers would flock to support a boy with the name Caesar.

Octavian gathered support from these veteran soldiers as he crossed from Apollonia to southern Italy, and then traveled north to Rome. As he went, he learned more about his great-uncle's death and the tense situation in Rome. Marcus Brutus and Cassius, the leaders of the plot to kill Caesar, had been pardoned for the sake of keeping order. Caesar's friend Mark Antony was consul and was taking over in Rome. He controlled all of Caesar's papers, including his will, although copies of the will were available and confirmed what Caesar had intended regarding his great-nephew. Some politicians, led by the elderly statesman Marcus Tullius Cicero, were trying to move away from the one-man rule instituted by Caesar and to restore the republic. Everyone was moving very cautiously. It was onto this scene that Caesar's heir appeared.

Young Octavian began by approaching Mark Antony. The biographer Plutarch, who lived in the second century AD, describes their meeting in his *Life of Antony:*

> He immediately greeted Antony as a friend of his uncle and reminded him of the property in Antony's safe-keeping. For each Roman was owed 75 drachmas under the arrangements of Caesar's will. Antony at first, thinking little of him because of his youth, told him that he was not thinking straight.

Antony was not the only Roman to underestimate the young Caesar. In this rejection we see the beginnings of a conflict between the two men that had far-reaching effects.

Despite the lack of help from Antony, Octavian began to fulfill the terms of his adopted father's will. This involved dispersing a sum of money to every Roman citizen, so it gained him a great deal of popularity—especially when he let it be known that he was financing it himself because Antony was slow to release Caesar's funds. Octavian also held some athletic games to celebrate Julius Caesar, and something very unusual happened. The historian Suetonius, in his *Life of the God Julius*, tells us:

A star shone for seven days continuously, rising at about the eleventh hour, and it was believed that it was Caesar's soul as he was received into heaven.

This star is now thought to have been a comet, but it had a profound effect on the Romans. It was certainly one of the reasons that Julius Caesar was later made a god. When the Senate officially deified Caesar in 42 BC, Octavian was able to call himself by another title—*divi filius*, "son of a god." Divine ancestry became another weapon in Octavian's struggle for power.

THE RISE TO POWER

Octavian wasted no more time on Antony for the time being and formed a friendship with Marcus Tullius Cicero instead. Cicero had always been a supporter of the republican style of government. He did not see eye-to-eye with Antony and had supported Brutus and Cassius. The young Octavian found himself friends with a man who had approved of Caesar's murder! But Cicero proved very useful. He was a public speaker of considerable ability, and his series of speeches against Antony in the autumn of 44 BC

An artist's reconstruction of the decorative painting on the ceiling of Augustus's house.

did a great deal to turn public opinion against Antony. Antony was forced to set off for his province in northern Italy toward the end of the year.

At the end of 44 BC, Antony's consulship expired, and Octavian found out that Cicero was quite capable of going against the rules of the republic when it suited him. Cicero ensured that the young man was allowed unheard-of privileges. He was allowed to join the Roman Senate at a very young age, and he was given the powers of a praetor. Cicero kept up his barrage of hostility toward Antony in the Senate. Octavian eventually found himself assisting in an expedition to fight Mark Antony in northern Italy. He was nineteen years old. Like Antony, Cicero had underestimated him. Cicero is reported to have said of Octavian:

Laudandum, ornandum, tollendum
(Praise him, flatter him, flatten him)

In this campaign, Octavian enjoyed two advantages. First, he had the name of Caesar, and second, his youth prevented people from realizing just how ruthless and ambitious he really was. When both consuls were killed during the campaign against Antony, Octavian took over the army, marched back to Rome, and demanded the consulship. The biographer Suetonius writes:

> When he was nineteen he took over the consulship by moving his troops threateningly close to the city of Rome, and by sending men to demand the consulship in the name of the army. And when the Senate hesitated, a centurion called Cornelius, the leader of the party, drew back his cloak and displayed the hilt of his sword, saying in the Senate-house without any hesitation, "This will do it if you don't."

A Roman aqueduct, used to bring freshwater into the city

Octavian himself tells a simpler, more flattering story. In his own *Res Gestae*, the account of his deeds written long after this time, Augustus the emperor says of himself as Octavian the young general:

The people made me consul when both consuls had fallen in battle.

Octavian had heard of the less than flattering comments Cicero had made behind his back, and he decided that Cicero was not to be trusted anymore. Octavian felt no particular loyalty to Cicero or the Senate, and contacted Mark Antony. Together with another Roman politician, Lepidus, he and Antony met and decided to take control of Rome. They passed a law announcing themselves as a committee of three, a triumvirate, and said they were going to restore the republic.

The triumvirs set themselves up legally using the law-making process of Rome, but they decided among themselves which one would hold the consulship for the next five years. They also controlled all the troops in the empire. They began their rule by killing and exiling all who stood in their way. Among the victims of this purge were Antony's uncle and Lepidus's brother, both of whom escaped into exile, and Cicero, who at the age of sixty-three was murdered as he tried to flee. The official name for this purge was proscription. According to Cassius Dio, Antony ordered that Cicero's head and hands be cut off and displayed in the center of Rome as:

> A sight to make the Romans shiver, because they thought they saw not the image of Cicero's face so much as the image of Antony's soul.

THE STRUGGLE WITH ANTONY

Between March 44 BC and November 43 BC, Gaius Julius Caesar Octavianus had risen from obscurity to fame as Caesar's heir and had gained the consulship of Rome at the extraordinary age of nineteen. He had made an alliance with Antony and Lepidus, by which the three men took over the government of Rome.

There was no time for Gaius Octavian to contemplate his achievements. He had to keep consolidating his relations with Rome and her army, and one of the best ways to do that was to show that he was still mindful of his adopted father. To the Romans, duty to one's parents was very important. That Gaius Octavian was not Caesar's natural son did not matter. He still had to show filial piety. In his *Res Gestae*, it is clear that avenging Caesar was now a priority.

A bust of Mark Antony, who was first Augustus's ally and then his enemy

I drove into exile the men who slaugh-
tered my father, gaining reparation for
their crime by the due course of law. I
later defeated them twice in battle as they
waged war against the republic.

Octavian used the support of Lepidus and
Antony to pursue Brutus and Cassius and
defeat them at the Battle of Philippi in 42 BC.
Once he had avenged Julius Caesar, he made a
solemn vow that he would build a temple in
Rome dedicated to Mars the Avenger, the
Roman god of war. You can still see the remains
of this temple in the heart of modern Rome.

Octavian now found that it was no longer
possible to restore the republic properly and
retire from public life. He was still only twenty-
one and a triumvir. He had youth and ambition,
and he now turned his attention to the other
members of the partnership.

It was clear that Lepidus provided nothing
more than a buffer between the two real
forces in the triumvirate, Antony and
Octavian. He was an ineffectual person,
always wavering before inevitably making the
wrong choice. When he and Octavian were
working to rid the seas of a pirate called
Sextus Pompeius, Lepidus made an attempt to

upstage Octavian and completely failed. He was forced out of office.

Octavian and Antony spent the ten years after the Battle of Philippi circling each other cautiously. Antony spent a good deal of time in the eastern end of the empire, while Octavian looked after the west and Italy. One crisis was weathered in 41 BC when Antony's wife, Fulvia, and his brother Lucius Antonius led a rebellion in Italy while Antony was away. Octavian had to deal with this and did so effectively—some said even brutally. Lucius Antonius took refuge in the Italian town of Perusia, which Octavian besieged and captured. Suetonius tells us what happened:

> When Perusia was taken, he punished many people, answering every one of them, as they tried to ask for pardon or to excuse themselves, with one reply, "You must die."

Antony himself was seriously embarrassed by his brother and wife, for he had not known what they intended. He and Octavian had to meet to patch things up. Antony married Octavian's sister Octavia as a sign of good faith. As the years passed, however, it became apparent that a crisis was approaching. Antony and Octavian could not exist as equal rulers of Rome for much longer.

The crisis came to a head when Antony embarked on an affair with Cleopatra, the queen of Egypt, and sent home Octavia. Octavian considered it an insult. Antony was rarely in Italy, and Octavian played on this by spreading rumors that Antony

Queen Cleopatra VII as depicted by a Roman artist

was living an extravagant life in Egypt. The Romans, priding themselves on their hard-working and austere lifestyles, did not react favorably to the idea that one of their greatest generals was growing soft in the East. Octavian's masterstroke was to find and read out the will that Antony had left in Rome. In it, Antony made his children by Cleopatra his heirs. He had abandoned his Roman wife and Roman children.

This wall carving depicts Roman galleys and their oarsmen.

Octavian now prepared for war. During the previous decade, his troops had successfully faced threats from the people of the Balkan area of Europe and from the navy of Sextus Pompeius. Octavian and his supporters were now experienced in warfare. Octavian's friend Marcus Agrippa had shown real skill as a general, and under his supervision a huge naval base was constructed in the Bay of Naples. Ships were prepared and men trained, and in 31 BC, Antony and Octavian met in a sea battle near the western coast of Greece, at a place called Actium. A poet of the Augustan Age, Virgil, gives us a glamorous description of Octavian in *The Aeneid:*

> Here was Caesar Augustus, leading Italy into battle, standing on the prow of his ship, accompanied by the Senate and people, the gods of the family and the great gods, a double light streaming from his face and his father's star shining over him.

Octavian won the Battle of Actium. Antony and Cleopatra fled to Egypt, abandoning their fleet. The historian Velleius Paterculus sums up the shame Romans must have felt when he says:

An Egyptian carving of Cleopatra from the Temple of Hathor in Dendera, Egypt

Cleopatra takes the first prize for running away. Antony preferred the company of the fleeing queen to that of the fighting soldier.

In Rome, Marcus Tullius Cicero, the son of the man Antony had killed thirteen years earlier, became consul. All statues of Mark Antony were removed.

The Battle of Actium did not produce total victory for Octavian. He first had to deal with mutiny among his troops, and then he had to pursue Antony and Cleopatra back to Alexandria, Cleopatra's headquarters in Egypt. In the end, both Antony and Cleopatra committed suicide when Alexandria fell, and Octavian was free to take over Egypt. He had Cleopatra's son by Julius Caesar, Caesarion, put to death. Octavian had no intention of sharing his precious legacy as Caesar's son with anyone else. Antyllus, son of Antony and Antony's first wife, Fulvia, was also put to

This Roman carving depicts children at play.

death. But Antony's other children—Iullus Antonius, son of Antony and Fulvia; and Cleopatra, Alexander, and Ptolemy, children of Antony and Cleopatra—were not judged to be a threat because they were too young. They needed a home and, surprisingly, the woman Antony had rejected, his wife Octavia, took them in to add to her own four children. That Octavia managed this large brood when there was so much potential for hurt and embarrassment says a lot about her.

By conquering Egypt, Octavian had transformed the economy of the Roman world. Egypt was very rich, and Octavian himself became very wealthy. Egypt also supplied Rome with a great deal of wheat, and Octavian decided to take Egypt officially into the Roman Empire to ensure the supply of this wheat. So much money entered into the Roman economy after the invasion of Egypt that interest rates on loans went down to a third of what they had been!

Eventually, in 29 BC, Octavian returned to Rome and celebrated. Once more he had to be careful about Antony, for it would have been very tasteless to celebrate a victory against a fellow Roman. On three successive days, Octavian held processions, known as triumphs, to celebrate three victories: his campaign in central Europe, and the conquests at Actium and Alexandria. A triumph was a military honor awarded to a successful general by decree of the Senate. The general and his soldiers would march through Rome, cheered by the people, and make sacrifices to the god Jupiter in thanksgiving for their victory.

Velleius Paterculus gives a very enthusiastic summary of the state of the *res publica*, the republic, under Octavian:

> There is nothing man can ask from the
> gods, nothing the gods can offer man,

This mosaic shows a Roman galley full of soldiers traveling down the Nile River in Egypt.

nothing a heart can desire or good fortune bring to pass, that after his return to the city Augustus did not accomplish for the res publica, the Roman people, and the world.

THE PRINCEPS

Over the years of struggle, Octavian had not faced crises alone. He had brought together three important and influential people to help him. First, there was his friend the general, Marcus Vipsanius Agrippa. Agrippa was a soldier and an organizer, but not a leader. He was content to play the vital role of second-in-command, without, it seemed, resentment or a desire for more power. Gaius Maecenas was a very different person. While Agrippa organized the army and navy and led them into battle, Maecenas kept his finger on the pulse of Rome, alerting Octavian to swings in public opinion and giving advice. These two very different men were ideal companions for Octavian, working for him without threatening him. Finally, there was Livia.

A bust of Marcus Vipsanius Agrippa, Augustus's general, trusted friend, and son-in-law

Livia was a remarkable woman, particularly in a society in which women had little official power and few rights. Her marriage to Octavian had caused a minor scandal in 42 BC. The historian Tacitus tells us:

Caesar, inflamed with passion for her, took her away from her husband. It is not known whether or not she was unwilling, and he was so eager that he took her into his home while she was still pregnant, without even waiting for her to give birth.

Octavian had already divorced his first wife, Scribonia, just as she gave birth to their daughter, saying that he was tired of being nagged. But Suetonius says of Octavian's feelings for Livia:

He loved her and respected her above all others to the end of his life.

As for Livia herself, she gave some useful advice when asked later how she maintained her influence over her husband:

Livia Drusilla, who Augustus married after divorcing his first wife, Scribonia

She answered that she was completely faithful, did whatever pleased him with good humor, never interfered in his business, and pretended to neither hear of nor find out about his "bits on the side."

Octavian and Livia had no children of their own, but Octavian's daughter from his former marriage, Julia, had several children. Octavian, as we shall see, valued these grandchildren highly and even adopted some of them to give himself heirs.

LAYING THE FOUNDATIONS

Now the four of them—Agrippa, Maecenas, Livia, and Octavian—planned the consolidation of Octavian's power. The turbulent past had to be buried, and people had to be persuaded to look forward. The celebratory triumphs helped to cheer the people, and other commemorations took place. Octavian founded a city at Actium and called it Nicopolis (victory city), while in Rome an arch was built in the Forum Romanum, a civic center with temples, shops, a Senate house, and speakers' platforms. The Romans used huge arches as memorials to great events, placing them in prominent positions and decorating them with carvings and statues.

Along with the celebrations came reminders of the blessings of peace, and the Senate took an important step here. Augustus himself in the *Res Gestae* says proudly:

Our ancestors had decided that when peace had been achieved on land and sea throughout the whole empire of the Roman people the Temple of Janus should be closed. In all the time from the foundation of Rome to my birth, according to tradition, this had happened twice. The Senate decreed it should be shut three times during my time as leading citizen.

Octavian also finished a building project started by Julius Caesar, a new Senate house in the Forum. There were games, gladiator fights, and animal hunts as part of the celebrations. The historian Cassius Dio says that this was the first time that Rome had seen a rhinoceros or hippopotamus.

In 29 BC, Octavian took on a very difficult task—that of checking the credentials of the men in the Senate. Traditionally this job fell to an official called a censor. It was necessary to make sure that the Senate was composed of men of the right sort of birth and wealth, and that senators behaved in a way that was fitting for their rank. A censor also had the power to make sure that the Senate was filled with men who would be supporters of that censor in the future. This would be very important if that censor wanted to enact some extraordinary measures, as Octavian planned to do. According to Dio, fifty senators quietly withdrew from the Senate and a hundred and forty others retired under compulsion. Octavian also introduced

This section of a larger Roman mosaic portrays a rhinoceros hunt.

the rule that senators could not travel outside Italy without permission. Now Octavian could always be sure where potential opponents were.

In 28 BC, Octavian enacted a law that invalidated everything he had done while a triumvir! Suetonius says:

> Since in the period of civil strife and wars he had enacted many deeds that went beyond the law and justice, especially when he had ruled jointly with Antony and Lepidus, he abolished all these in one law.

This seemed like a very dangerous admission from Octavian. Was he inviting people to criticize him for acts of the triumvirate such as the proscriptions? Making this law was probably Octavian's way of showing the Roman people that the bad old days were gone and could be forgotten. Certainly, with the abolition of the triumvirate's deeds, Octavian was ready to move onto his most important reform.

THE SETTLEMENT OF POWER

Octavian's official power had rested in two positions: the consulship, which he held continuously from 31 to 23 BC, and the triumvirate, now abolished. But he had many other sources

Other changes were made as Augustus and his friends gradually acquired more power and as circumstances forced change. In 23 BC, for example, Augustus resigned the consulship and did not feel the need to hold it continuously again. He had realized that by holding one of the two consulships every year, he was blocking one way in which senators could gain glory and fulfill ambition for themselves. A plot against him, formed by some dissatisfied senators, probably encouraged him to think of this way of appeasing the Senate. Instead of the consulship, Augustus took the office that appealed to the people—an honorary tribune. He was not one of the ten official tribunes, but he enjoyed all the powers of a tribune for the rest of his life. These powers included the right to propose a law without having to consult the Senate. Augustus also assumed authority over all provincial governors so that he could intervene anywhere in the empire, not just in those provinces that he personally supervised.

Augustus was seriously affected by an unknown illness in 23 BC. Dio describes a touching sickbed scene in which Augustus gathered the leading men of Rome around him and gave his ring to Agrippa. This was very significant. A Roman nobleman's ring held his

seal, a carved gem that when imprinted in wax left an impression on important documents. It served as a signature does in

One of the signet rings of Augustus, a symbol of imperial power, used to make an impression on official documents to confirm their authenticity. Augustus gave this ring, or one like it, to Agrippa when he felt that he might die without an heir.

legal documents today. When Augustus gave his ring to Agrippa, he put him in charge of official documents. Augustus recovered from this illness, but it raised a troublesome question for everyone: What would happen to Rome now if Augustus died?

PERSUADING ROME

Augustus was often referred to as the princeps, from the Latin word meaning "leading citizen," a term that under the republic had been applied to the most respected senior senator. An important aspect of Augustus's rule was his desire to keep up the appearance of republican forms of government. The Senate still met and debated and made recommendations. The people still gathered to hold elections every summer. Laws were passed, and the courts adjudicated cases. Augustus himself held no power that could not be traced back in some way to the political forms of the republic. And yet no one doubted that things were definitely different. Augustus transformed the republic into the empire, but encouraged the notion that nothing had really changed.

Augustus advanced the idea that Rome was following the old traditions, and this is made clear in the laws he passed, the building schemes that were undertaken, and the literature that was produced during his rule. In these schemes, Augustus also managed to do a lot of good for ordinary Roman

This Roman silver coin with the head of Augustus was found in the Teutoburg Forest of Germany, where in AD 9 the Roman general Varus and three of his legions were massacred by Germanic tribes.

people, although he was not successful in everything he tried. One of his greatest failures was the campaign against the Germanic tribes of northern Europe. The Germanic tribes put up a stiff resistance to Roman expansion. In AD 9, a general called Varus foolishly ventured too far into hostile territory and three entire legions were massacred—a disaster for Rome and Augustus, although both recovered.

Augustus himself was not so popular that no one disagreed with him, and he found, as many leaders do, that there were a few people willing to make attempts on his life. None of these men succeeded, and it is difficult to tell

An artist's depiction of the Forum Romanum, the administrative and political center of Rome during the time of Augustus

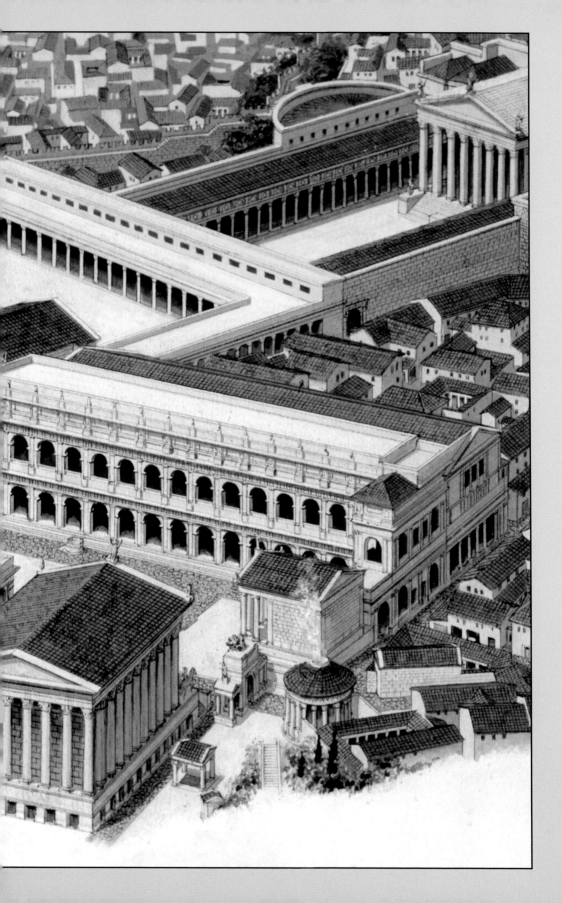

how serious a threat they really were. Also, Augustus's personal life was occasionally very unhappy. But none of this detracts from his achievements. Augustus made changes in practically every aspect of Roman life, from passing a law to encourage an increase in the birthrate to having a channel of the river Tiber cleared of rubbish and widened to avoid flooding. He promoted his popularity with the citizens of Rome by handing out money, staging games, and constructing and refurbishing buildings. In the *Res Gestae*, he writes:

> According to the terms of my father's will, I gave out three hundred sestertii to each man of the Roman people. In 29 BC, in my own name, I gave four hundred sestertii from the spoils of war. Again, in 24 BC, I gave out four hundred sestertii to each man, and in 23 BC I made twelve donations of grain bought at my own expense. In 12 BC for the third time I gave four hundred sestertii.

To give you an idea of what kind of wealth this represented, an ordinary soldier in Augustus's time was paid 900 sestertii a year. To buy enough corn to feed that soldier for a year would cost about 240 sestertii. Augustus's handouts were sufficiently generous so that an ordinary family could buy enough basic food for several months.

Augustus also initiated a new building boom. As he says in *Res Gestae*:

> I built the Senate-House and the Chalcidicum next to it, and the Temple of Apollo on the Palatine, along with its colonnades, the temple of the God Julius . . . I completed the Forum of Julius and the basilica which lies between the Temple of Castor and the Temple of Saturn, works which had been begun and abandoned by my father . . . In 28 BC, at the decree of the Senate, I repaired eighty-two temples in the city, and left out none that needed repair at the time . . . On land which I bought at my own expense, I built the Temple of Mars Ultor and the Forum of Augustus, using the spoils of war.

These building projects occupied prime land in the center of Rome and sometimes involved years of building. The Temple of Mars Ultor, which Augustus vowed to build at the Battle of Philippi in 42 BC, was not completed until 2 BC.

This nineteenth-century woodcut depicts the Temple of Mars Ultor, begun by Augustus after he defeated Caesar's assassins at the Battle of Philippi. Mars was the Roman god of war, and Mars Ultor means "Mars the Avenger."

Suetonius tells us that Augustus never hid his enjoyment of the games and gladiatorial shows. In this he was like most Romans. In *Res Gestae*, Augustus writes:

I put on gladiatorial games, three times in my own name and five times in the names of my sons or grandsons. About ten thousand men fought in these games . . . I put on hunts of African wild animals twenty-six times, in circus or forum or amphitheater, either in my own name or the names of my sons or grandsons.

We do not have to rely on Augustus's own words to be convinced of the material benefits Rome enjoyed under his rule. Many of the stories Suetonius tells us about Augustus illustrate the range of measures in which he was personally involved.

He invented a system of guarding against fires carried out by night-watchmen . . . He took upon himself to repair the

Flaminian Way as far as Ariminum, and divided up the other road repairs to be done by men who had celebrated triumphs, to be paid for out of the wealth they had gained in war . . . When there were complaints about the short supply and high price of wine, he said very sternly, that his son-in-law Agrippa had made sure that men would not go thirsty by providing several aqueducts . . . He made his Forum rather narrow, because he did not go as far as to force the owners of the nearest houses to leave.

And, sure enough, if you go to Rome today, you will be able to walk around Augustus's Forum and see the ingenious way in which its architect hid the irregularities in the plan of the building—irregularities forced upon Augustus by the recalcitrant, or resistant, homeowners nearby. What Suetonius does not say, but what you will be able to see for yourself, is the very high wall that Augustus had built between his Forum and those houses, as a firebreak perhaps, or to keep out of sight those who had thwarted the princeps.

Certainly the Forum bordered the Subura, one of the slums of Rome, where fires were

The Forum of Augustus today. On the left is the high wall that Augustus built as fire protection or to hide from view the slums and commercial areas of the city.

frequent. But Augustus was very good at using his buildings to make statements. This very Forum contained a temple to Mars, the god of war (here called Mars Ultor, or Mars the Avenger), to remind people that Augustus had avenged the murder of his adopted father, Julius Caesar, at the Battle of Philippi. The Forum also held countless statues of Rome's heroes from bygone days and, of course, a statue of Augustus himself in front of the temple in the center. Augustus might have made a pretense of being just an ordinary man, but he expected no one to take him seriously about this.

THE ART OF SELF-PROMOTION

One of Augustus's most famous sayings, recorded by Suetonius, was that he found Rome a city of brick and left her a city of marble. This is an exaggeration, of course, but Augustus was right to be proud of his achievements. The work was not just decorative. The construction of aqueducts and a new set of public baths built by Agrippa must have had an impact on people's health. But there is no doubt that Augustus and Agrippa were determined to leave a permanent mark of stone on Rome. One such monument is worth discussing in further detail, to show how Augustus could make use of such buildings to promote himself.

The Ara Pacis Augustae is a very grand name meaning the "Altar of Augustan Peace." We hear of it in the *Res Gestae*:

The Ara Pacis Augustae, or Altar of Augustan Peace, the construction of which began in 9 BC. It is built of white Italian marble and is covered with relief sculptures.

When after a successful expedition to Gaul and Spain I returned to Rome in 13 BC, the Senate decreed that an altar of Augustan Peace should be consecrated on the Campus Martius, to give thanks for my return.

The altar was finally finished in 9 BC. It stood outside the old city walls, in the area north of the city called the Campus Martius (Field of Mars), close to the main road into the city center, the Flaminian Way. It still stands on a bank of the Tiber River, moved a little way from its original position and partially restored by Italian archaeologists. The altar is

A relief sculpture from the walls of the Ara Pacis. The woman with the two children may be Venus Genetrix, the mother of the Julian family and symbolic mother of the Roman Empire.

guarded on all sides by a wall, which is full of carvings and sculptures on both sides, with the most impressive scenes on the outside.

One outside wall shows an elegant and elaborate carving of the spindly stems and leaves of an acanthus plant curled into beautiful patterns. Among the leaves, small animals and

insects hide at just the right height for children to make a game of spotting them, and carved swans clap their wings overhead. Above this is carved a procession of people—priests and senators and members of Augustus's family—on their way to an important ritual, probably the sacrifice that dedicated the building of the altar itself in 13 BC. Some of the people are solemn; some are chatting with each other. A young woman and her husband are being "shushed" by the old lady next to them. Children walk with their parents, one little boy anxiously hanging onto the cloak of the man in front of him so that he doesn't get lost. Augustus himself is walking with the priests while Agrippa, who, in 13 BC, married Augustus's daughter, Julia, leads the family of the princeps. Augustus and Agrippa are easy to spot because they look like their portraits on coins, while the lady behind Agrippa is surely either Livia or Julia. Some of the faces are extremely realistic. One elderly senator in particular looks straight out at the viewer with a rather fed-up look on his face, as if he is tired of the ceremony already.

On either side of the entrances to the altar are carved panels. In one panel, the legendary hero Aeneas makes a sacrifice upon reaching Italy. Aeneas supposedly escaped the destruction of Troy by the Greeks and came to Italy, where his descendant Romulus founded Rome. Romulus is also carved on the wall. Augustus was trying to convey the idea that he, too, was a founder of a new Rome. On another panel, a beautiful woman representing either the earth or the land of Italy sits amidst the fruit and the animals produced by the land, with two babies in her lap. The message here is clear—prosperity is returning to Italy under Augustus.

Here, many visitors to Rome would have had their first sight of Augustus, and it would have reminded them of the things that Augustus held dear—respect for religion, family values, and Rome's great past. There is one more trick to the altar. Nearby, on the Campus Martius, Augustus had set up a huge sundial, the pointer of which was an Egyptian obelisk. The shadow of this obelisk moved across a diagram etched on paving stones on the ground to tell the date and time of day. On Augustus's birthday, the tip of the shadow lay in the doorway of the Ara Pacis as a tribute to the builder. But beautiful though it was, the greatest symbolism lay in its name— the Altar of Augustan Peace.

A POET IN THE SERVICE OF THE STATE

While architects improved the look of the city, cultural life was also flourishing. Augustus's friend Maecenas had been gathering a collection of gifted writers who were encouraged to use their talents in certain directions, which they were happy to do. The outstanding writer of this group was the poet Virgil, still regarded as one of the all-time greats of Western literature. Virgil's writings unashamedly celebrate the theme of Augustan peace and glorify Augustus himself. Today we might find it discomforting for a poet to glorify a politician, but we must remember that to many Romans the Age of Augustus was a welcome relief from the grinding years of war and poverty.

In one of his earliest poems, from a collection called *Eclogues*, we find out that Virgil had a special reason to be grateful to Augustus.

This Roman mosaic portrays the poet Virgil with two muses, goddesses who inspired poets and singers.

In this poem, a young shepherd tells his friend that the family farm, which was confiscated from him, was returned to him by a young man. This had happened to Virgil's own family in the past. Augustus was still Octavian then, and the triumvirs were doing a fair amount of military campaigning. This meant that they needed a great deal of land on which to settle retired soldiers. The confiscation of land took place all over Italy, and many people were simply thrown off their farms to make way for the soldiers. Virgil was lucky. Augustus's friend Maecenas returned his family's farm, and so the poet recorded his gratitude.

Virgil's greatest poem is *The Aeneid*, a long poem telling the story of the Trojan prince Aeneas. Centuries earlier, the Greek poet Homer had told the story of the Trojan War in his poem called *The Iliad*, and this would have been well-known to every Roman schoolchild. Virgil wrote *The Aeneid* as a kind of sequel to *The Iliad*, and it told the story of Aeneas's escape from Troy and his wandering around the Mediterranean before landing on the shores of Italy. There is no doubt that Virgil intended his readers to make comparisons between the hero of his epic and Augustus. In several prophetic passages, Aeneas is given a glimpse into the future of the nation he will found. In one such passage, Virgil glorifies the Roman Empire and the Augustan Age:

> Other peoples will more delicately coax living shape out of bronze, will draw out real

faces from marble; they will plead cases better, will trace out the course of the heavens and foretell the rising of the stars. You Roman, make it your place to rule over the peoples with your empire and—these are your particular skills—to place tradition upon peace, to spare the conquered, and crush the arrogant with war.

Peace was not just something to be enjoyed by the Romans under Augustus. It was their duty to bring it to the world, by conquest if necessary. Augustus had brought a sense of destiny to his people.

FAMILY MATTERS

In 2 BC, Augustus received a special honor. The Senate awarded him the title of *pater patriae*, "father of the country." This was a great honor, and according to Suetonius, Augustus had tears in his eyes when he accepted it, saying:

> Fathers of the Senate, as I have achieved my dearest hope, what else have I to ask of the immortal gods except that it is allowed that I keep this universal backing of yours to the very end of my life.

Augustus was sixty years old in 2 BC, and with this title it appeared that he had everything. Rome was stable and prosperous, and there was peace in the empire. The temple to Mars in the great Forum of Augustus had

GERMANIA

GAUL

ETRURIA

Massilia

Via Flaminia

Perusia

Roma

Via

Nola

HISPANIA

SARDINIA

SICILI

AFRICA

Boundaries of the Roman Empire ··················

THE ROMAN EMPIRE AT THE TIME OF AUGUSTUS

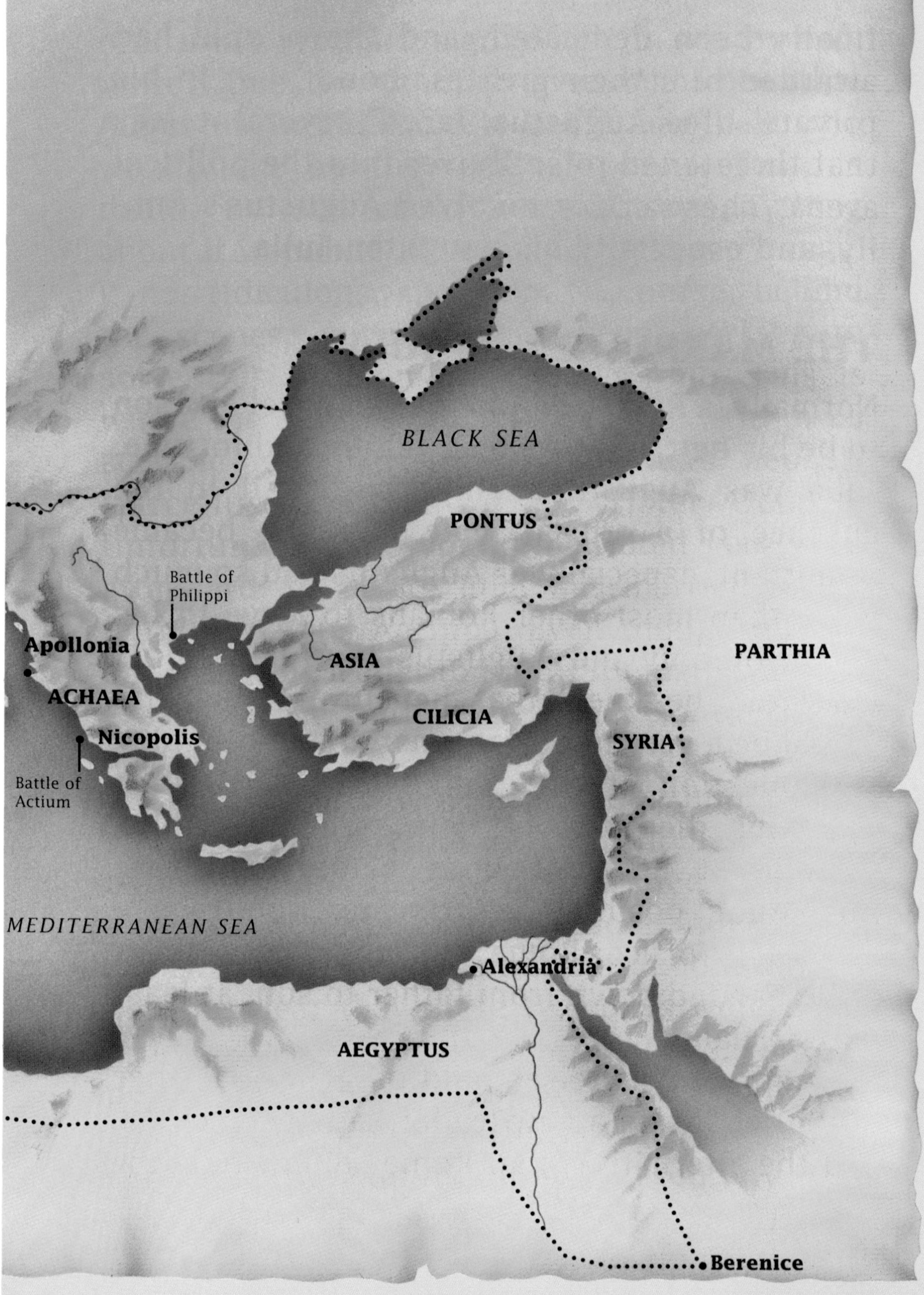

BLACK SEA

PONTUS

Battle of
Philippi

ASIA

PARTHIA

Apollonia

ACHAEA

CILICIA

Nicopolis

SYRIA

Battle of
Actium

MEDITERRANEAN SEA

Alexandria

AEGYPTUS

Berenice

Germanicus, who was adopted by Tiberius at the insistence of Augustus. Augustus wanted to ensure there would be enough heirs to the throne.

considered but did not measure up to Augustus's standards. Augustus was looking much further ahead. Although Tiberius already had a son called Drusus, Augustus made him adopt another son, Germanicus, the eldest child of Tiberius's brother Drusus. After the deaths of Lucius and Gaius within eighteen months of each other, Augustus was taking no chances. He wanted to ensure that there was another generation of the imperial family already in place.

Augustus was widely reported to have disliked Tiberius, and there is evidence for this in his reluctance to make him his heir until there was no other option. Countering this supposition are the letters Augustus wrote to Tiberius, which show nothing but affection. When news came of the disastrous defeat of

The family of Augustus. From left to right, Augustus, Drusus, Livia, and Tiberius.

three Roman legions under Varus in Germany in AD 9, Rome was facing a real crisis. The effect on the people of Rome was very powerful, and Augustus himself cried out to the inept general who had lost so many men, "Quinctilius Varus, give back my legions!" Tiberius was the one who set out for Germany and brought the situation under control. This was a critical display of his authority to Augustus and to Rome. His right to succeed Augustus was thus confirmed, although, as we shall see, there was a small string attached to Augustus's will.

The obelisk that Augustus erected at the eastern end of the spina, or central barrier, of the Circus Maximus

Augustus the Man

What about Augustus the man? We do not have a lot to go on here because Augustus himself wrote very little that survived. Fortunately, some Romans were as curious as we are about the private man behind the public face, and the historian and biographer Suetonius was one of them.

He had bright and shining eyes, and liked to have it thought that there was some sort of divine power in them. He was pleased if someone at whom he looked rather sharply dropped their gaze as if at the brightness of the sun. When he was old, he could not see so well out of the left eye. His teeth were spaced out and small and not too nice. His hair was

CHAPTER 7

wavy and fairish; his ears of an ordinary size. His nose jutted at the top and turned down at the end. His coloring was between dark and fair. He was short, but so well-proportioned that it was not noticeable, unless someone taller were standing next to him . . . He was not as strong in his left hip, thigh, and leg as his right, and often limped because of this.

In many ways, Augustus took care to live a very simple life. He liked plain, everyday food like

bread, fruit, fish, and cheese. He was also very careful not to drink too much wine. He wore clothes that had been woven in his own household by Octavia, Livia, or Julia, or by one of his granddaughters. Suetonius says, rather disapprovingly:

An artist's reconstruction of the Circus Maximus during a chariot race. At left is Augustus's obelisk.

The modesty of his household goods and furnishings is clear even now from those tables and couches that are still around, most of which are only just fit for a private citizen.

Even in his speech, Augustus kept to what was plain and simple. Like everyone, he had some favorite expressions, faithfully noted by Suetonius. Some of these have a very homely ring to them, such as the phrase "quicker than boiled asparagus" to express something that happens very speedily, or, to express that he was feeling listless, "I feel like a beet root."

THE PATRON

The world of a Roman politician was a very open one. Every morning, there was a daily ceremony called the *salutatio* (the greeting). People who were under an obligation of some kind to Augustus would regularly call at his house on the Palatine Hill, in a system based on patronage, which means soliciting the support of a powerful or wealthy person. This system worked at all levels of society. The man under the obligation was called the client, and the

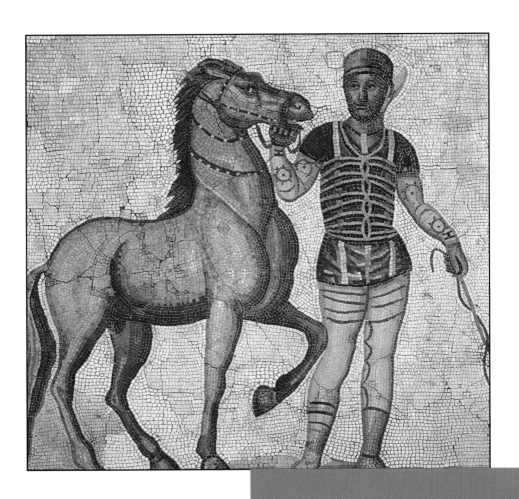

This Roman mosaic depicts a charioteer wearing his team colors.

man visited by clients was the patron. Augustus, at the top of the heap, was a patron to the whole of Rome, and many people would call to ask for favors. It was an accepted part of Roman society that the patron's house would be open in the morning for these clients to call, and Suetonius tells us that Augustus was no different:

> His morning salutatio was open to everyone, even the common people, and he

This wall carving shows the winner of a chariot race receiving his trophy.

would listen to the requests of those who came with such friendliness that, when one man was hesitating over handing him a request, Augustus gave him a mock-reproof saying, "It's as if you were giving a penny to an elephant."

REFORMING THE ROMANS

On the whole, Augustus seemed able to cope very well with being the focus of such attention. He once wrote to Tiberius, who had clearly been upset by some gossip:

Don't give in to your youthful impulses and complain too much that someone is saying nasty things about me. If no one is doing nasty things to us, that is good enough.

But one disadvantage of this openness was that Augustus's personal life was often in the limelight, and in one area in particular it caused some problems. Augustus had decided early on to do something to reform public morals. In 18 BC, for example, he passed laws that tried to encourage people to get married, stay faithful, and have children. Some Romans may have resented Augustus for trying to do this, for as Suetonius sorrowfully says:

> Not even his friends deny that he committed adultery, though they excuse him by saying that he did it not out of lust but deliberate intent to find out more easily what his opponents were planning, using their women.

However his friends excused him, Augustus does not appear in too good a light here. The Senate enjoyed a neat revenge on him, according to the historian Dio, when he was telling them to keep their wives in order.

This stone carving portrays gladiators fighting wild animals in the Circus Maximus.

He told them, "You ought to advise and to order your wives in the way you like—that's what I do." On hearing this they bothered him all the more, wanting to know what advice he gave Livia.

No doubt the last thing Augustus was prepared to do was share details of how he kept a lady as formidable as Livia in line. When he had tried to reproach Mark Antony over his affair with Cleopatra, Antony replied in very forthright terms:

What's made you change your tune? My affair with the queen? She's my wife. After all, have I only just started it or has it been going on for nine years now? Are you sleeping with just Livia? If, by the time you read this letter, you haven't had Tertulla or Terentilla or Rufilla or Salvia or all of them, then good luck to you. Does where or who matter?

THE DEATH OF AUGUSTUS

1
2
3
4
5
6
7

CHAPTER 8

The Age of Augustus was viewed by later Romans as Rome's golden age. Augustus led a long, hard-working life, which in the end was dedicated solely to his city and the structure of political power he established. Everything and every-one else along the way was sacri-ficed when Rome demanded that sacrifice—Cicero, Antony, Julia; friends, enemies, and family. Augustus was single-minded, and that single-mindedness meant that he must have been a lonely figure, the only man at the top of the pyramid of power he had built. He had outlived most of his friends—Octavia, Agrippa, Maecenas, and Virgil—by many years.

He died, as we have seen, at the age of seventy-five in the town of Nola, near Naples. His body was brought from Nola to

Rome, with the lead-ing men of each town carrying it in relays.

Rome's grief was extravagant. Augustus had a magnificent funeral, and his remains were laid to rest in a huge tomb called a mau-soleum, which you can still see today on the banks of the river Tiber. Like his uncle, Julius Caesar, he was deified.

Among his papers Augustus left the *Res Gestae*, instructions for his funeral, a state-ment of the position of the empire, and his will. He left money to be handed out to the Roman people and to the army, and he made his stepson Tiberius the major beneficiary of his will. Poor Tiberius did not get the support he might have expected, however, for

This Roman mosaic shows workers crushing grapes in a wine press. Both wine and olives were important exports for Roman trade.

in his will Augustus made Tiberius his heir by saying:

> Since cruel fortune has robbed me of my sons Gaius and Lucius, I make Tiberius Caesar my heir.

There is nothing like knowing you were the second choice. This is one of the reasons why many people since have thought that Augustus disliked Tiberius. And Tiberius went on to earn one of the worst reputations of all the Roman emperors.

Livia was granted the title Augusta to honor her long marriage to Augustus. She lived for fifteen more years and was deified in 41 AD. Augustus and Livia had no children together, but through Tiberius, Drusus, and Julia their grandchildren and descendants ruled Rome for several generations. First came Tiberius, then the grandson of Drusus and Antonia, Emperor Gaius, known to us by his childhood nickname, Caligula. After Gaius came Claudius, the elderly and lame son of Drusus and Antonia, assumed by most of Rome to be rather stupid because he suffered several disabilities. Finally, Augustus's great-great-nephew, the emperor Nero, died without

This section from a larger mosaic portrays the harvesting of olives.

an heir, and the dynasty of Augustus and Livia, called the Julio-Claudians by modern historians, died with him.

The title "Caesar" has lived on into modern times in the titles "Kaiser" and "Czar." That is not Augustus's only legacy to the world. Virgil's poetry is studied the world over. The architecture of Augustan Rome has had a great influence on much of Western culture. The eighth month of the year is still called August in the Western world. The consolidation of power that Augustus brought about was a logical outcome for a civilization that, even as a republic, drew its resources from conquered peoples. Rome's real power came from her legions and the ambitious men who commanded them. Augustus was the first such man to take all political power for himself and hold on to it. But in the process, he created the "glory that was Rome."

A NOTE ABOUT SOURCES

The *Res Gestae* is a very important source for information on Augustus's life because it tells us what he wanted us to know and what he thought was important. A few of Augustus's letters and sayings have also survived.

Augustus was also written about by a great many people in the ancient world. The most important is Suetonius, who wrote about the first twelve leaders to take the name Caesar. In the second century AD, Suetonius worked for the emperor Hadrian as a secretary for a time, so he had access to all sorts of records kept in the Imperial Archives. The period of Augustus's rule was also covered by later historians like Dio and Tacitus.

We also have some written material from people like Cicero and Velleius Paterculus, who were alive during Augustus's lifetime and even took part in the events of the period. Cicero

The jobs on this ladder were quaestor, aedile, praetor, and consul.

dictator An office under the republic that was only used in an emergency. The person chosen as dictator had absolute power, but only six months in which to get the state back on its feet.

equites The Latin word meaning "knights." Originally the cavalry of the Roman army, the equites became the class below the senatorial class. Often, equites were wealthy men who ran the businesses of Rome.

Forum Romanum Usually just called the Forum, this was the heart of Rome. It was a low-lying flat area where temples, law courts, and the Senate House were all grouped together.

legion A unit of the army, usually about 5,000 to 6,000 men.

obelisk An upright, four-sided stone pillar that gradually tapers and is topped by a pyramid.

praetor The second office from the top of the *cursus honorum*. The work of praetors usually involved supervising the law courts. After his year in office, a praetor might go on to govern a small province.

princeps "Leading citizen," a title by which the emperor was addressed.

proscription The announcement that a man is condemned to death (or exile, if he flees).

province An area of the Roman Empire ruled on behalf of the Senate and people of Rome by a governor.

quaestor The lowest office on the *cursus honorum*. The work of a quaestor was usually that of assisting a more senior official, perhaps in a province or treasury.

res publica The public affairs of state; in other words, the government of Rome, the republic.

salutatio A morning ceremony in which clients would visit their patrons.

Senate A group of advisers. To qualify for the Senate, you had to have money and be of good birth, and you had to have been elected by the people of Rome. Your family was then part of the whole senatorial class, the upper class in Rome.

tribunes of the people Elected every year to safeguard the interests of the ordinary people of Rome, they had the very important power to propose legislation, although the people had to approve the legislation by voting for it.

FOR MORE INFORMATION

ORGANIZATIONS
American Classical League
(National Junior Classical League)
Miami University
Oxford, OH 45056
(513) 529-7741
Web site: http://www.aclclassics.org
e-mail: info@aclclassics.org

American Philological Association
University of Pennsylvania
292 Logan Hall
249 South 36th Street
Philadelphia, PA 19104-6304
(215) 898-4975
Web site: http://www.apaclassics.org
e-mail: apaclassics@sas.upenn.edu

Classical Association of New England
Department of Classical Studies
Wellesley College
106 Central Street
Wellesley, MA 02481
Web site: http://www.wellesley.edu/
  ClassicalStudies/cane
e-mail: rstarr@wellesley.edu

WEB SITES

Due to the changing nature of Internet links, the Rosen Publishing Group, Inc., has developed an online list of Web sites related to the subject of this book. This site is updated regularly. Please use this link to access the list:

http://www.rosenlinks.com/lar/august/

FOR FURTHER READING

NONFICTION

Connolly, Peter. *Pompeii*. London: Macdonald Educational, 1979.

Moatti, Claude. *The Search for Ancient Rome*. New York: Harry N. Abrams, 1993

Suetonius. *The Twelve Caesars*. New York: New American Library (Penguin-Putnam), 1993.

FICTION

Graves, Robert. *I, Claudius*. Harmondsworth, England: Penguin Books Limited, 1953.

Lawrence, Caroline. *The Thieves of Ostia*. London: Orion Children's Books, 2001.

Sutcliff, Rosemary. *The Eagle of the Ninth*. New York: Farrar Straus Giroux, 1993.

BIBLIOGRAPHY

PRIMARY SOURCES

Appian. *Roman History: The Civil Wars.*
Cambridge, MA: Harvard University
Press, 1979.

Augustus. *Res Gestae.* Oxford, England:
Oxford University Press, 1967.

Cassius Dio. *The Roman History.*
Cambridge, MA: Harvard University
Press, 1924.

Cicero. *Philippics.* Oxford, England:
Clarendon Press, 1900.

Ehrenberg and Jones. *Documents
Illustrating the Reigns of Augustus
and Tiberius.* Oxford, England:
Oxford University Press, 1976.

Paterculus Velleius. *History of Rome.*
Cambridge, MA: Harvard University
Press, 1979.

Plutarch. *Life of Antony.* London:
William Heinemann Ltd, 1920.

Suetonius. *The Lives of the Caesars.*
London: William Heinemann Ltd, 1924.

Tacitus. *The Annals.* Oxford, England:
Clarendon Press, 1897.

Virgil. *The Aeneid.* London: William Heinemann Ltd, 1946.

SECONDARY SOURCES

Chisholm, Kitty, and John Ferguson, eds. *Rome, the Augustan Age.* Oxford, England: Oxford University Press, 1981.

Jones, A. H. M. *Augustus.* London: Chatto & Windus, 1977.

Southern, Pat. *Augustus.* London: Routledge, 1998.

Syme, Ronald. *The Roman Revolution.* Oxford, England: Oxford University Press, 1960.

Webster, Graham. *The Roman Army.* Chester, England: Grosvenor Museum Publications, 1973.

INDEX

ABOUT THE AUTHOR

Fiona Forsyth studied classics at Somerville College, Oxford University. She now teaches classics at the Manchester Grammar School in England.

CREDITS

EDITOR
Jake Goldberg

LAYOUT
Geri Giordano

SERIES DESIGN
Evelyn Horovicz